2360	Eser	Su Sesi
	Yazar:	Cevat Çapan
	Yayıncı:	Arc Publications
	Ülke:	İngilizce

THE VOICE OF WATER

the Voice
of Water
CEVAT ÇAPAN

Translated by Ruth Christie
with an introduction by
Ronald Tamplin

PUBLICATIONS
2017

Published by Arc Publications,
Nanholme Mill, Shaw Wood Road
Todmorden OL14 6DA, UK

978 1910345 67 2 (pbk)
978 1910345 68 9 (hbk)
978 1910345 69 6 (ebook)

ACKNOWLEDGEMENTS
These poems were first published in Turkish as
Su Sesi (Yapı Kredi Yayınlan, Istanbul 2013).

The translator is deeply grateful to Cevat Çapan
for supplying background information to several poems;
to Jean Boase-Beier for her editorial expertise and
succinct suggestions; to Selçuk Berilgen for his knowledge
of all things Turkish; and to her husband James,
as ever her link to the computer.

Design by Tony Ward
Printed in Great Britain by T.J. International Ltd,
Padstow, Cornwall

Cover picture: Tony Ward

Arc Publications gratefully acknowledges financial support
for this book from the Republic of Turkey,
Ministry of Culture & Tourism (TEDA).

Supported using public funding by
**ARTS COUNCIL
ENGLAND**
LOTTERY FUNDED

**Arc Publications Translation series
Series Editor: Jean Boase-Beier**

CONTENTS

Introduction / 9

to Tuncay Çavdar
Tuncay Çavdar'a

Cevat Çapan's poetry is somehow seamless. To enter into its texture, its fabric, you can start almost anywhere, and you are soon released into his world. Take the closing lines of 'The Fisherman Talks to a Mermaid' (p. 27):

A woman talks to herself in the kitchen
as she descales a fish, and by her
a child looks at the mountains in his atlas.

The scene is at once real and visionary, a world of her work and the child's imagining, of home and journey, of absorbed intimacy and letting go. Or again, in 'No Return' (p. 73), a man tells a child the story of his own father's long voyage – "I loved to begin that amazing story in the middle..." – and it leads them, both child and man, through many seas and lands, until

At the day's end I'd say to Bünyamin, 'don't forget
these sailors – captains and their crew –
would see such enchanted places in those distant lands
their eyes would be so dazzled they would lose their way
and could never go home again.'

Throughout, events, landscapes, encounters, relation-ships, feelings, memories, seem to enshrine their opposites, sometimes to resolve them in unity, sometimes to lament that as impossibility, more often to hold them in suspension, even in extremity, as "hope against hope". It is a savouring of the stuff of the world in all its aspects. And this is achieved with an economy of expression that is exemplary. What seems to be autobiographical broadens to include the reader, not as intruder but in some way involved and subsumed in the event. We find and recognise ourselves, possessed by the poet's recall in a commonality of self-knowledge.

Beyond this summary listing then, I'm choosing a number of poems or themes which seem to me to embody this sense of Çapan's pervasive achievement. I'll begin, perhaps obliquely, with music. "I hum folksongs I know by heart under my breath, / all night as I wait for you" he says in 'Yalıoba Diary II' (p. 87), and in 'Ney' (p. 33) – the haunting Turkish reed flute – he describes how a man's "... tobacco-tanned fingers searched / for those distant bygone tunes." In 'Why This Unknown Smoky Haze?' (p. 65), "the echo of an old song sounds" in his ears and "A woman... / hums a folksong, the words forgotten." In 'Gramophone Record' (p. 41)

> ... resting under a plane-tree
> Hafız Burhan
> Hears himself sing that air you love,
> "Birdsong all over the plains".

In the minatory 'Watch your Ps and Qs, My Friend' (p. 69) there are more singers: "These last days we've been living in a world of sounds; / Deniz Kızı Eftalya, Hamiyet Yüceses", more records again, by two celebrated singers from the past, and now "Children's eyes are on the skies, on flying birds, / their ears on birdsong", and then at the end of 'Haydar Haydar' (p. 81), "Birdsong unceasing / in the branches of trees."

Folk music is deep in the Turkish psyche and here it is blended into the poems, pulsing through them, fully remembered or with its words forgotten, beneath the breath, as it repeats on records or as it spreads wide from its origin, indomitable in the birds of the air at song. Such elemental music is a key to memory, probably so in all cultures. I think of *fado* in Portugal; of the Elizabethan Sir Philip Sidney in his 'Defense of Poesy' – "I never heard the old song of Persie and Douglas, that I found not my heart moved more than with a trumpet"; of Bessie Smith and the Blues, and of the actress Susannah York's beautiful remark about Irish music as she heard it played by The Chieftains – "It gives me memories I never had." The late Talat Sait Halman spoke of "the continuing presence of the past" that this Turkish heritage brings with it. Çapan is heir to that and it is a sustaining presence in the poems here, always with him, in story, event and emotion. And as we read we are invited into this world of sound, each in our own way, as he writes, however personal or from another world it is. These are memories, ours to be taken, by virtue of a kindred humanity. That, centrally, is the way of poetry.

Another key determinant in Çapan's writing is colour. I think it is so in poetry generally. The atmosphere of colours habitually seen lends its softness or its intensity to the different landscapes we inhabit, much as it does with painters: van Gogh in Northern Europe, then transformed in the South of France. Much of Turkey's colour is intense, seas and the skies the deepest blues. But, in the poems here, I would want to highlight one particular poem where colours work more as synaesthesia than simply as visual sensation, 'Correspondence' (p. 25). It begins

> For a while they exchanged letters in colours
> they loved,
> translating to each other the feelings that chimed
> with the colours.

Within the poem a number of colours are elaborated – "golden-brown", "flesh-coloured", "orange", "purest white" of snow, "green" of the shadow cast within the snowfall. Others are implied – in their letters the correspondents "... researched the names of darkness / in different tongues / and with what colours night became silent." But the controlling colour, the thread which runs through the poem is "blue", modulating finally into an embodiment of it, "the lapis lazuli stone" and the word for it "in Babylon" – 'uknu'. As it progresses through the poem, blue gathers to itself a number of qualities. First, "the blue that suddenly appears from steel under water, / does it evoke loneliness or distance?". Next:

In a play, blue is the colour of nobility,
      quoth
The Knight of the Sorrowful Face, the colour
      of nobility and distance.

– and then the enigmatic last stanza,

In Babylon,
they divide male and female into two species
they call the *lapis lazuli* stone
      'uknu'.

In this exchange of letters between two people, "loneliness or distance", "nobility", "nobility and distance", are all conditions gathered into the colour blue, which is finally given another name in a different language. There are other gatherings here too. The Knight of the Sorrowful Face is Don Quixote but what he says comes from the role he is given in Tennessee Williams' *Camino Real*. In its opening sequence he says: "Blue is the colour of distance and nobility and that's why an old knight should always have somewhere about him a bit of blue ribbon" to remind him of "the distance he has gone and the distance he has to go." Çapan encapsulates in one the old romantic knight, comic yet heroic, battered but still battling, and the modern despair and horrors of the Camino Real redeemed as they may be with the knight's assertion which ends the play: "The violets in the mountains have broken the rocks!". As enigmatic, but equally revealing, is Çapan's own conclusion to 'Correspondence' which introduces two pieces of seemingly disconnected information about ancient Babylon, the division of "male and female into two species" and then their word for the blue stone *lapis lazuli*, 'uknu'. Is the sequence of "letters in colours" in the poem aiming to overcome separation, loneliness and distance between a man and a woman, a distance, perhaps in miles, perhaps too, as sometimes in all relationships, in feeling, symbolized by an ancient notion of two distinct species? And what of the word 'uknu'? Why did the Babylonians call the blue stone that, and why does Çapan draw our attention to it? It bears no relationship to the Turkish for *lapis lazuli* but there is a word given in the standard *New Redhouse Turkish Dictionary* – 'uknum' – which would seem to have some relation to 'uknu', cognate if not the same. It is listed as 'Arabic, Learned', and its meaning 'basis, root: substance'. Perhaps then, the concealed meaning here is philosophically something like 'essential nature', implying the union in one nature of male and female, not a division into two species. And so the various blues within the poem resolve, and so too any division by distance or feeling in the letter-writers themselves is resolved by their unity, in one secret word, untranslated because mysterious, untranslatable.

Lapis lazuli was, from the fourteenth century, ground up into powder to give vivid pigment to painters. It is an easy move then from that to the substantial element in poems of picture-making. We often forget that the root of the word 'imagination' is the Latin 'imago' – picture. The medieval *vis imaginitiva* was the power of making pictures in the mind, shaping inwardly what we see outwardly in the world and giving it back again to the world in another clarity. Cevat Çapan does this supremely. His work is full of pictures, a mind interpreting the world by matching it inwardly in his mind, so we can see both mind and world vividly and simultaneously. In 'Days of the Population Exchange' (p. 83) for example:

Deep in sombre thought they gazed at the land ahead,
was it here, in this fire-ravaged place, they would begin new lives?
With artillery bunkers between squat bushes,
half a hillside covered with olives, blasted by dynamite,
fragments of rock ground to dust in a cement factory.

It is at first sight a straightforward account of people caught up in the population exchange between Greeks and Turks that, in 1923, ten years before Çapan was born, followed on from the War of Independence – it involved around two million people, here individualized to a single loaded boat. Historical and sight-laden it is, but poetry works through

13

the local to the universal. We see what Çapan shows us and we incorporate it with other daily sights, hopes and fears. History repeats itself and so does suffering. In 'Nightmare' (p. 53), other and different faces are "... half-erased from a dream, / drawn by a shaky hand on a tumbledown wall" and

Now a shepherd sits by a stream
rolling his cigarette,
mountains rise in the distance,
ruins are sunk in sand
and shrines without altars
remain under water.

There is much of dream in these poems and of nightmare and between these poles, the elusive and open-ended. Here there's the shepherd, absorbed almost meditative in ordinary action, beside the stream, natural, flowing, sustaining, the constant but distant mountains, and our endeavours, past, sunk, and shrines, their meanings gone from them, submerged in that greater water towards which the stream still flows. Where indeed are we now? The poems are tense with meaning.

Turkey is in many ways a country pivotal between East and West and this is true, politically and geographically, and perhaps, even now, at a crossroads it has visited many times before. But that tends to neglect what Turkey is in itself, to see it somehow horizontally, neither this nor that, and not as a deep land in itself, to be viewed as it were vertically, lived in, fought over, layered with successive civilizations, religions and languages. Homer, Aristotle, St Paul were here before they were absorbed into what we call the West. The buildings of Venice took Byzantine shapes. The capacity to give and to receive is as strong today. When we see Çapan reflecting in his poetry Cervantes, Tennessee Williams, Lorca, Man Friday and so on, we should not now see this as some influence from the West but as recognition of what is kindred and given to all.

Equally with Li Po, Scheherezade, Isfahan; these are not various degrees of the East but gifts in balance with other gifts. It was not till I met and translated with the Turkish poet Coşkun Yerli in Ankara, that I attempted haiku, impressed by his. The Japanese form seemed to fit my own realization and glimpses of Turkish landscape, long journeys through towns with ancient names, storks nesting on the chimneys, Phrygian sites. Later the Irish poet Biddy Jenkinson suggested I fuse my separated images into longer forms. This is how things work. I see this same kind of fusion magisterially, in Çapan's lines in 'Yalıoba Diary II' (p. 87):

> In my hand, so many silences echoing in its hollow
> a little seashell,
> slowly I bring it to my ear
> to listen to Li Po's lines.
> A Buddhist monk is climbing
> to a distant cloud-capped peak –
> today on the eighteenth of July,
> in an empty oakwood
> we expect the cicadas.
> Like old eagles memories circle
> leaving black specks
> in a deep blue sky

– four haiku-like realizations, fused as one thought-narrative. A final poem, as full, is 'Zurbaran' (p. 103):

> Red glow within darkness.
> And every tone of green fades
> disappearing from sight lost
> and between light and shade
> radiance reaches its peak.
>
> Do you remember Ali of Nurgana?
> his memories concerning Lorca
> from Seville and from Cadiz?
> Now and then he painted abstracts
> that reminded us of Selim Turan.

There are enigmas here. What does the first verse describe? Who is Ali of Nurgana? Why Zurbaran? Selim

Turan was a Turkish painter who painted abstracts, as the poem tells us. The first verse, in fact, looks like a fine description of one of his paintings – abstract, a picture in words of a painted picture. As for Ali of Nurgana, like many things in poems, the poem works for us without knowing every last detail. The poem tells us all we need to know – this is part of a conversation, with a friend or friends, or a letter maybe, about Ali who had memories of Lorca from Seville and Cadiz and now and then painted pictures that remind them of Turan's painting. This intimate kind of exchange is so typical of Çapan's poetic method. It is autobiographical in tone, but it transfers itself to us without the need to know more than he gives us. But why the seventeenth-century Spanish painter Francisco Zurbaran? There are large collections of his paintings in Cadiz and in Seville where he lived and worked. Çapan tells us in 'Yalioba Diary II' that he visited Seville with friends in 1964; the hotels were full and the five of them slept in the one car. It's perfectly possible too that they saw a lot of Zurbaran's paintings. One of his characteristics was his liking for, and skill with, white paint and the play of light. Here I might be fanciful. Zurbaran might be simply a painter Çapan recalls when he thinks of Seville but it may be – I like to think it is – that he intends a contrast between the painter of the title and Selim Turan, the painter whose picture is in the first verse. If it is so, then this is a connection as well as a contrast. White light played through a prism separates into its component rainbow colours just as a canvas primed with white is the base for all the colours an artist can use. In 'Correspondence' snow "etched the tree-branches to purest white", and there was "a green shadow gliding to every root". Is this bringing together of Zurbaran and Turan another 'essential nature', an 'uknu' between white and colour, baroque and modern abstraction, in the way Çapan sees this world of things?

To telescope a bit some extended remarks of Paul

Valéry, "all poetry is translation", this insofar as it renders gatherings of pre-existing things into gatherings of words, the role of language itself, the naming of things. Sadly we can't say translation is always poetry. Very happily, Arc Publications has done immense service transmitting compelling Turkish poetry to us, publishing in the past Cevat Çapan's *Where Are You, Susie Petschek?* in Michael Hulse's fine translation and now *The Voice of Water* as given us by Ruth Christie, consummate and vital translator of Turkish poetry and prose alike over many years. Her versions ring true to Cevat Çapan and to poetry itself. Many and grateful thanks.

Ronald Tamplin

THE VOICE OF WATER

I

FROM WHERE WE ARE NOW

RÜZGÂRLA

Neler gizler bu kuyunun derin dibi,
gören göze neler yansır o suskun
    karanlıktan?
Mermer kasnağına abandığında?

"Kara göründü!" diye bir ses miydi
umutsuz çalkandığın enginde duymak
    istediğin?
Yıllarca deniz! deniz! diye sayıkladığında?

Kucaklaş bu ormanın kararan yeşiliyle
artık karaya vurmuşken nasılsa.
    Nerdeydin?
bunca zaman, nerelerde, hangi kuytuda?

Uçan bir tüydü izlediğim
    birlikte savrularak
        erişmek için bu menzile
           sonunda.

IN THE WIND

What lurks in the depths of this well,
what is reflected in the seeing eye from
    the silent dark
when you lean over the marble rim?

Was there a voice shouting 'Land ahead!'
that you wanted to hear on your rocking
    hopeless horizon?
Didn't you rave for years in your sleep
    for the sea, the sea?

Embrace the darkening green of this forest
now that you've struck land.
    Where were you?
Where on earth, all this time, where hidden?

It was a floating feather I followed
    flung in the air together
        to reach this harbour
            at last.

MEKTUPLAŞMALAR

Bir süre sevdikleri renklerle yazışmışlar
        birbirleriyle,
renklerle ilgili duygularını birbirlerine
        aktararak.
Kızıl kahverengi bir kuş kanadı neler
        anlatmış olabilir,
ve çeliğe su verilince birden beliren mavi
yalnızlığı mı çağrıştırır, yoksa uzaklıkları mı?

Bir oyunda, soyluluğun da rengidir mavi,
        diyordu
Mahzun Yüzlü Şövalye, soyluluğun
        ve boşluğun rengi.

Karanlığın değişik dillerdeki adlarını
        araştırmışlardı sonra
ve gecenin hangi renklerle sessizleştiğini.

Ten rengi bir kumsalda uyanmıştım bir sabah,
turuncu bir güneş doğuyordu denizden.

Hiç unutmam, bir kış gecesi, kar yağmıştı
        inceden,
bembeyaz kesmişti ağaçların dalları,
yeşil bir gölge süzülmüştü her ağacın
        dibine.

Erkek ve dişi diye iki cinse ayırırlar
ve "uknu" derlermiş lacivert taşına
        Babil'de.

CORRESPONDENCE

For a while they exchanged letters in colours
        they loved,
translating to each other the feelings that chimed
        with the colours.
A golden-brown birdwing could tell
        so many tales,
and the blue that suddenly appears from steel under water,
does it evoke loneliness or distance?

In a play, blue is the colour of nobility,
        quoth
The Knight of the Sorrowful Face, the colour
        of nobility and distance.

Later they researched the names of darkness
        in different tongues
and with what colours night became silent.
I woke up one morning on a flesh-coloured beach,
an orange sun was rising from the sea.

I'll never forget, one winter night, a light
        snowfall
had etched the tree-branches to the purest white,
a green shadow gliding to every tree root.

In Babylon,
they divide male and female into two species
they call the *lapis lazuli* stone
        'uknu'.

DENİZKIZIYLA KONUŞAN BALIKÇI

Denizin tuzlu suları karardığında,
"Fısılda bana adlarını," diyor balıkçı
   denizkızına,
"halayıkların olan o renkli balıkların.
Sanma ki bu ilk kaçışım
içinden çıkılmaz kargaşasından karaların.
Çarparak köpüklü dalgalarına gerçeğin
   kayalarının.
Uyandır beni ve hatırlat heyecanını yeniden
   orman yangınlarının."

İnce bir yağmur soğutuyor şimdi
kararan çamların sıcak küllerini
ve külrengi bir bulut ufuk uzayıp giden.

Yalnız deniz görünüyor kıyadaki evin
   penceresinden,
duyulan yalnız dalgaların sesi martıların
   eşlik ettiği.
Bu yosun kokusu mu meltemle gelen,
kuruyan zeytin dallarıyla yakılan ateşten?

Bir kadın kendi kendine konuşuyor mutfakta
balığın pullarını ayıklıyor bir yandan,
bir de bir çocuk, atlasındaki dağlara bakan.

THE FISHERMAN TALKS TO A MERMAID

As the salty waters of the sea grow dim,
'Whisper to me the names,' says the fisherman
      to the mermaid,
'of those colourful fish, your slaves.
Don't imagine this is my first flight
from the inextricable maze of shores,
clashing with foaming waves
      of rocky reality.
Rouse me, remind me again of the thrill
      of forest fires.'

Now a fine rain chills
the warm embers of blackening pines
and the horizon stretches to an ashen cloud.

Only the sea can be seen from the window
      of the house on the shore,
only the voice of the waves can be heard, matched
      by the seabirds.
Is this the smell of seaweed on the offshore wind,
from a fire lit with withered olive boughs?

A woman talks to herself in the kitchen
as she descales a fish, and beside her
a child looks at the mountains in his atlas.

DÖRT MEVSİM

I

Mayınlı tarlalarda topladığın gelincikler
parçalanan bir gövdenin kanlı serpintileriymiş
   gibi,
kaçarcasına uyanmıştın o düşten;
karanlıkta yolunu yitirmiş bir uyurgezerdin
   karşılaştığımızda.
Toprağın altından çıkarılmış bin yıllık bir yazıtı
   heceliyordum ben bir söğüdün altında.
Bir sabah dolaştığımız kırların serinliğiyle
   uzattın ellerini.
Bizi bekleyen kimse yoktu o sessizlikte:
   ne yerçekimi, ne rüzgâr.
Uçarak kaybolmuştuk gözden o sonsuz mavilikte.

II

O yaz duvar sıvadım durmadan;
malayla bir güzel yaydım harcı ateş tuğlalarının üstüne.
Su serpip perdahladım duvarı sıva kurumadan..
Akşamları ovada gün batışını seyrettim telgraf direkleri
   arasından.
Geceleri bir tren geçerdi şantiyenin önünden ışıklarla
   kaybolan.

FOUR SEASONS

I

The poppies you picked in the minefields
were like a spray of blood from a dismembered
   body,
you awoke in flight from that dream;
you were a sleepwalker, you'd lost your way in the dark
   when we met,
while under a willow tree I was figuring out
   a thousand-year-old inscription from underground.
One morning you held out hands cool as the wilderness
   where we loitered.
No one was waiting for us in the silence:
   no gravity, no wind.
As we flew in the endless blue we were lost from sight.

II

That summer I kept plastering the wall;
spreading a fine plaster on the fire-tiles with my trowel.
Spraying water, I polished the wall before it dried..
At evening between the telegraph poles I watched
   the sunset over the plain.
At night a train would pass the yard, its lights
   lost in the distance.

III

Denize ulaşmam uzun sürdü, geride kaldı bozkır, tozlu
   kamyonlar.
Yıkık tapınaktan sonra bembeyaz deniz feneri iki limanlı
   burunda.
Bahçede güz gülleri. Bu sessiz buluşmayı kutsuyor denizin
   sesiyle rüzgâr.

IV

O kış yalnızlığımıza sığındık. Çakan fener de bizdik,
uğuldayan deniz de. Bizimdi kumsaldaki ayak izleri,
Bizdik açmayı bekleyen çiçek avludaki saksıda.
Bizdik onaran aramızdaki yıkık köprüleri o kış uykusunda.

III

My affair with the sea was long, the country and dusty trucks
    were left behind.
After the ruined shrine the snowwhite lighthouse
    on the cape with two harbours.
Autumn roses in the garden, Wind blesses this silent meeting
    with the voice of the sea.

IV

That winter we sheltered in our solitude. We were the flashing lighthouse,
the roaring sea. Ours the footprints on the sand.
In the courtyard we were the flower in the pot ready to open.
We were the broken bridges between us healing in winter sleep.

NEY

Giderek tenhalaşan köşende
tütünden sararan parmaklarınla
o uzak ezgileri arardın geçmişten
göllerden koparılmış kamışta.

Söğütlerden süzülen serinliğinde
akşamın
dağlar da seni dinlerdi gölgelenen
yamaçlarında,
dağlar da, dereler de, uzayıp giden
ovalar da.

Zaman gölünün bir kıyısından
dallardan örülmüş bir salla
sürüklenip gelirdik geçerek
eski teşrinlerden, soğuk kânunlardan
soluğunun büyüsüyle bir hızla
özlediğimiz
haziran sıcağına.

NEY

In your slowly dwindling corner
on a reed plucked from the lakes
your tobacco-tanned fingers searched
for those distant forgotten tunes.

In the evening cool filtered through
      willows
the mountains heard you on their
   shady slopes,
mountains and valleys, and far-reaching
      plains.

Drifting on a raft
woven of branches from a shore
on Time's lake, we came
urged by the magic of your breath
and passed the old Octobers, cold Decembers
         on to the longed-for
               warmth of June

HAMİŞ

Düşünde
bir yanardağın lavları içinde
doruğa tırmanıyormuş,
    seninle
        el ele.

FOOTNOTE

In your dream,
through a volcano's lava
she climbs to the peak
        hand-in-hand
                with you.

KALDIĞIMIZ YERDEN

Yaşadıklarının bir tortusuydu o masum anılar,
geleceği nerdeyse unutulmuş bir zamana
    bağlayan.
Unutma, belleğin zindanındı senin,
düş gücün özgürlüğün.
Böylece dolaşıp durdun bir süre
dilini anlamadığın insanlar arasında,
gökyüzünün mavi bir yama gibi
görünüp kaybolduğu gökdelenler altında.

Nasılsa rastlamıştın bir gün ücra bir bitpazarında
gözden çıkarılıp bir köşeye atılmış o tozlu
    yadigârlara
ve anlamıştın hemen, derinden bir acıyla,:
aldırışsızlık da bir çeşit rahatlamaymış
    sonunda.

Şimdi gene bir sürgündesin kendinden,
uyandığın yer uyuduğundan başka.
Sen de duymuşsundur elbet eski bir kulağı kesikten:
kendini kolay kolay bağışlayamazmış insan.

Innocent memories were the grounds of your life,
    binding
the future to a season soon forgotten.
Don't forget, your memory was your prison,
Your dream your strength and freedom.
So you travelled abroad and stayed a while
among people whose language you didn't understand,
below skyscrapers where the sky came and went
like a blue patch.

Once in a remote fleamarket you came upon
those dusty keepsakes, tossed in a corner
    out of sight,
and bitterly deep down you realized:
indifference too was a kind of peace
    at last.

Now you are still in exile from yourself,
your waking and sleeping are two different worlds.
Surely you must have heard of the old adage,
Forgiving ourselves isn't easy for humankind.

İLAHİ SU KUŞU

Bizim bir yanardağımız olsa
külleri büsbütün soğumamış
biri bize bir kahve yapsa
o soğumamış küllerde

Oturup aşağı ovaya baksak
sen orası Çukurova'dır desen
ben, hayır, o ova Ahmatova, desem,
ondan şiirler okusak.

Bizim bir kuş evimiz olsa
içinde bir de kış köşesi
uzun kış gecelerinde
yaz sabahlarını özlesek

Bir de rüzgârgülümüz
ne zaman gündoğusu esse
bize tâ İsfahan'dan
gül kokusu getirse

Ya davul tozu, minare gölgesi?
Onlar şimdi Issız Ada'ya
yazlığa gitmişlerdir,
benim gözümün bebeği,
ciğerimin köşesi.

WHAT A SILLY QUESTION!

Suppose we had a volcano
its ashes not quite cold
and someone made us coffee
in those dying embers

Suppose we sat and looked down at the plain
and you said that's Çukurova
but I said, no, it's Ahmatova,
and we read her poems.

If we had a tiny birdhouse
within it a winter corner
where on long winter nights
we'd yearn for summer mornings

And when the east wind blew
our weather vane would bring us
from far Isfahan,
the scent of roses

Was that all moonshine and shadows?
Light of my life,
my darling,
they must have gone now to their summer place,
the Desert Island.

TAŞ PLAK

Karlar eridi,
     suyun serinliği bu, dağlardan inen;
Rüzgârı kesen de dağlar, doğan güneşi
     perdeleyen de.
Yamaç yeşerince, toz duman azalıyor
     şosede
Yol boyu çiçekleniyor meşeler
     arasında.
Yağmur dinerse, serçeler de duyulur
     yeniden:
Özlediğin o "kuş sesleri ovalara
     yayılır"
Ve bir çınarın altında dinlenirken
     kendini dinler Hafız Burhan.

GRAMOPHONE RECORD

The snows have melted,
    flowing down the mountains, water's coolness;
Mountains that cut off wind and veil
    the rising sun.
As slopes turn green, the highway's dust
    is laid.
The wayside springs into flower
    between the oaks.
When the rain stops, we hear the sparrows
    again:
And resting under a plane-tree
    Hafız Burhan
Hears himself sing that air you love,
    "Birdsong all over the plains".

BİR DAĞ MASALI

Her zaman gittiğim bir yer değil,
    geçerken uğramıştım.
Olanlar herkesin önünde olmuş,
gene de kimse anlamamış
    neden çıkmış o kavga.
"Gözünün üstünde kaşın var!" mı demiş
    biri öbürüne?
Öbürü, "Yok deve!" diye
    karşılık mı vermiş?
O güne kadar her şey can ciğer
    kuzu sarmasıymış oysa
        aralarında
Nedense kim vurduya gitmiş onları
    ayırmaya çalışan da.

A MOUNTAIN STORY

It's not a place I visited often,
        I saw it in passing.
What happened happened in public,
yet no one understood
        why the quarrel began.
"You've an eyebrow over your eye!" did one
        say to the other?
Did the other reply
        "Come off it!"?
All had been harmony up till then
        sweetness and light,
                but somehow or other
how the peacemaker got killed
        nobody knows.

RASGELE

Şimdi bir yaz gününü düşlüyordur martılar
mendirekten yangının alevlerine bakarak,
Salaş kahvenin duvarında silik bir manzara
durgun bir gölün sularına dalıp giden sevgililer,
sanki o bildik sonsuz iri güllere bakıyorlar.
Denizler durulmaz dalgalanmadan'ı mırıldanıyor
yaşlı balıkçı, gümüş oltasında çırpınan bir şiirin
ilk dizesi, "Ah kitapsız," diye inliyor, "arkası
gelmez ki bu meretin!" Aklında hep o yaz günü,
gülleri solmayan o bahçe, dinlemekten bıkmadığı
o şarkı, durmadan perende atan bir cambazdı o,
şapkasından üç tavşan çıkaran bir hokkabaz,
içinde büyümek istemeyen bir çocuk.
Oysa yaşlı bir balıkçıydı şimdi kıyıdaki yangının
alevleriyle ısınan, elindeki oltası yosunlara takılan.

Bu akşam bambaşka renklerle batacak
    denizde güneş.

RANDOM

The seagulls must be dreaming now of a summer day
as they gaze at the flaming fire from the breakwater,
as at a mural half-erased in the Salaş coffeehouse
of beauties diving in a lake's still waters,
they gaze at the endless huge familiar roses.
The old fisherman mutters at the restless waves
mounting before a storm, the first words of a poem
struggling on his silver line, "ignorant Philistine"
he swears, "the damned thing's stuck!"
Always in his mind that summer day,
that garden where the roses never faded,
that song he never tired of, an acrobat
turning continuous somersaults, a magician
conjuring three rabbits from his hat,
and in it a child who never wanted to grow up.
Now an old fisherman warming himself
by the flames of a fire on shore,
his fishing-rod stuck in the seaweed.

This evening the sun will sink in the sea
    with very different colours.

O UÇSUZ BUCAKSIZ DENİZLERDE

Diyelim bu senin son sabahın –
biri yavaşça fısıldıyor bunu kulağına;
sen de içine sindirmeye çalışıyorsun
    bu gerçeği
ve yavaş yavaş değişiyor bakışların.

Zamanla ilgili bir değişim bu.

Yaşanacak zaman, ölünecek zaman.

Gülümseyerek "Zaman halleder her şeyi,"
diyorsun kendi kendine.

Oysa ne zaman kalmıştır artık senin kendini
    bağışlayacak,
ne sevdiklerine selam yazacak bir kurşunkalem,

Sen gene de o sevdiğin atlasları aç,
gidemediğin adaların adlarını hecele
o uçsuz bucaksız denizlerde
son soluğunla.

Gece, gündüz, yaz, kış
ve araya giren baharlardı
hiç unutamadığım.

IN THOSE BOUNDLESS SEAS

Let's say it's your last morning –
somebody softly whispers this in your ear;
and you try to absorb
    the reality
and gradually your perceptions change.

A change to do with time.

Time to be lived in, time to be dead in.

Smiling, you say to yourself,
"Time resolves all."

But now there's no time left to forgive yourself,
and no lead pencil to write your dear ones a greeting.

So open again those atlases you loved,
and with your last breath,
recite the names of the islands you never reached
in those boundless seas.

There were nights and days, summers and winters
and seasons between
which I can never forget.

GİRİT

Akşamları
kapı önünde oturur konuşurduk
bekleyen yaşlı kadınlarla.

Bir daha döner miyiz diye
sorar gibi bakardı gözleri
koparıp savrulduğumuz yerlerden
kök saldığımızı sandığımız
   topraklara?

Bu esen yel
zaman denizinde
uzaklaşan adanın
tuzunu taşırdı çakıllı kıyılardan.

Turuncun rengi solardı
örtüleri havalandırmak için
çeyiz sandıklarını açtıklarında,
cibinlikler
denizin nemiyle
salınırdı balkonda...

Bir gemi belirir
kaybolurdu ufukta.

CRETE

In the evenings
we'd sit by the doorway and talk
with the old women waiting.

Their questioning eyes would ask,
shall we ever return
to the lands
we feel as our roots,
from where we were wrenched and displaced?

This wind that blows
would carry salt
from the pebbly shores
of an island distanced
in time's sea.

When they opened the bridal-chests
to air the garments
the orange colours would fade,
and mosquito nets
would sway on the balcony
in the damp sea-mist…

On the horizon a ship would appear
and vanish.

EVİNE DÖN KÜÇÜK KIZ

Akşamları kapının önüne oturup
o yaşlı kadınlarla konuştuğumuzda,
o kadar çok şey anlatılırdı ki anlayamadığım;
çekinerek sorardım neden çiçekli
saksılar yok diye pencerelerde.
Aralarında yün eğirenler, bir yandan
bir türkü tuttururlardı duyulmayan bir sesle.
Bazen de güldürmek için o yaşlı teyzeleri
adada kalan evimizde, dedem nargilesini
nasıl fokurdatır, onun taklidini yapardım
    yanaklarımı şişirip.

O saatlerde şehirden dönen amcaları
    getirirdi kaptıkaçtılar;
biz çocuklar koşar, bacaklarına
    sarılırdık o amcaların.

Hava kararırken koşarak eve dönerdim,
yolda rüzgârla konuşurdum korkudan.
Oysa birden ay çıkar,
yolun sonundaki denizi aydınlatır,
kurtarırdı beni gecenin zindanından.

GO HOME LITTLE GIRL, GO HOME

When we talked with those old women
who sat by their doors in the evening,
so much was said I didn't understand.
Why no pots of flowers at the windows
I'd wonder timidly. And then
the wool-spinners among them would begin
to hum a tune together under their breath.
Sometimes to raise a laugh in these old 'aunties'
in our island home, my grandfather would blow
narghile bubbles loudly, and I'd puff
    in cheeky mimicry.

Those days our 'uncles' were brought home
    from town by minibus,
we kids would run to clamber up
    their legs and cling.

With darkness falling I'd run home
and talk to the wind in panic all the way.
But suddenly the moon would appear
to light up the sea
at the road's end, and rescue me
from the prison of night.

KARABASAN

Eskiden, kırık değilken kanadın,
süzülür uçardın o dağın yamacında.
Çınarların gölgesine karışırdı
    dökülen tüylerin.
Adlarını bilmediğin eşkıyalar
at koşturur, tozu dumana katardı
    aşağıda ovada.
Bir eski zaman kuşuydun sen,
onlar bir masalın sonuna koşan atlılar.

Bir düşten yarı silik suretler bunlar,
yıkık bir duvara titrek bir elin çizdiği.
Kulağında hâlâ nal sesleri
uyanınca uzaklaşan –

Şimdi bir su başında oturmuş
cıgarasını sarıyor bir çoban,
uzakta yükselen dağlar,
üzeri kumlarla örtülü ören yerleri
ve sular altında kalan
sunaksız tapınaklar.

NIGHTMARE

In the old days when your wing was unbroken,
you would glide down the mountain slope.
        The feathers you shed
mingled with the plane-trees' shade.
Bandits whose names were unknown to you
raced their horses, in clouds of dust
        on the plain below.
You were an old-time bird
they were riders who raced to the end of a story.

These are faces half-erased from a dream,
drawn by a shaky hand on a tumbledown wall.
Hoofbeats still in your ear
that fade as you wake –

Now a shepherd sits by a stream
rolling his cigarette,
mountains rise in the distance,
ruins are sunk in sand
and shrines without altars
remain under water.

II

CORRIDORS OF MEMORY
BELLEĞİN DEHLİZLERİNDEN

ALATURKA

Gün batarken bir bekleme odasında
        buluyoruz kendimizi
birbirini tanımayan üç beş kişi.
Biri ıslık çalmaya çalışıyor
        kesik dudaklarıyla.
Saçlarını düzeltmeye çalışıyor yanındaki
        kırık parmaklarıyla.
Kimse bilmiyor kimi, neyi beklediğini.
Dışarda çiçekler açmıştır diye düşünüyor
köşede sessizce yere çömelmiş duran.
Sessizlik kulak tırmalıyor.
Birden, hafifçe açılan kapıdan
ölüm başını uzatıyor en baştan çıkarıcı
        gülüşüyle
aramıza katılmak için.

ALATURKA

Here we are in a waiting-room
        at sunset
a handful of people who don't know each other.
One tries to whistle
        through cracked lips.
His neighbour tries to comb his hair
with crooked fingers.
No one knows anyone or why they're waiting.
The one who stays quietly crouching in the corner
reflects that outside flowers are in bloom.
Silence grates on the ear.
Suddenly through the half-open door
Death sticks his head
        and with his most seductive smile
asks to be one of us.

Artık uçmayı özlemeyen kuşları seyrediyor
    penceresinden,
yangın yerinde oynayan çocukları.
Uçuşan küllerin arasında buldukları uçları yanık
kitapların sayfalarını karıştırıyor çocuklar.
Hava kararıyor kıyıda. Oysa karşı adada
batan güneşle kızarıyor kayalık yamaçlar.
Akşam mezelerini hazırlıyor olmalı Niko
    asmalı tavernasında.
Bu yakada Hasan Kaptan bir kızın adını yazdığını
    hatırlıyor
denize açıldığı ilk teknenin küpeştesine.
Bu kıyılar dar gelirdi ona o günler,
deniz hep uçsuz bucaksızdı oysa.
Başını döndürürdü o uzak denizlerden dönmek –
kime, neye döndüğünü düşünmek.

Durgun sularda ağır ağır yaklaşmak mı karaya,
yoksa azgın fırtınalarla boşuna boğuşmak mıydı
    yaşlanmak?

Artık uçmayı özlemeyen kuşları seyrediyor
geçmişe, şimdiye, geleceğe açık
    penceresinden.

FROM A SHORE

From his window
he watches the birds no longer keen to fly,
and children playing in the place of fire.
The kids stir up scorched pages of the books
they find in the flyaway ash.
On shore air darkens. But over there on the island
rocky hillsides glow in the sinking sun.
Nikolaki must be busy preparing the evening meze
       in his vinehung taverna.
Here Captain Hasan remembers how he wrote
       a girl's name on the bulwark
of his first boat that headed out to sea.
Those days he thought these shores too close,
the sea vast and endless.
The thought of returning from such distant seas –
to whom or what – it blew his mind.

To grow old,
was it to drift to land through turgid tides,
or to battle in vain with furious storms?

From his window
open to past and present and future
he watches the birds no longer keen to fly.

SAATLERI ONARMA ENSTİTÜSÜ
Edip Cansever'in anısına

O küçük kız yıllar önce
yeşil bir şişe getirmişti bana
içinde kırmızı bir cin.
Ne ben o cini azat edebildim
hemen,
ne geçen zamanın farkına vardım
onca yıl.

Nice yazlar sonra,
anladım ki,
iki kez yıkanamazmış kimse
aynı suda
ve ölüp gitmiş
göldeki o bildik kuğular.

Gene de arayıp duruyor çocuklar
bakarak sulara
bir göl kenarında.
Bilemeyecekler oysa
nelerin kaybolup gittiğini
soğuyan küllerin arasında.

THE TIME REGULATION INSTITUTE
In memory of Edip Cansever

Years ago a little girl
brought me a green bottle,
a red djinn inside.
I couldn't free that djinn
right away,
and for years
I never noticed time passing.

Summers later,
I realized
no one could bathe
in the same water twice
and in the lake the swans we'd known
were dead and gone.

Children still peer in the waters
by a lakeshore,
searching, searching.
But what is lost and gone
among the cooling cinders
they'll never know.

Durmadan göğe bakan bir adam.
Düşen bir uçak mı,
uçaktan uçan bir insan mı?
Belki de dağ başında bulunan
bir mektuptu aradığı.

İşsizlik yıllarında
kıdemli bir hukuk mezunu olarak
aylak bir arkadaşıyla
Muameleciler operetini yazmıştı
Muhlis Sabahattin'e özenip.

Alevler içinde bir deniz düşlerdi
Takfor'un meyhanesinden
Adalar'a baktıkça;
bu yüzden bir gece benzin döküp
denizi tutuşturdukları söylenir
mahallenin yaşlıları arasında.

Sağ kalan arkadaşları da hiç unutmazlar onu:
hem hızlı, hem dayanıklı
bir uzun mesafe koşucusuydu ne de olsa
bir ara da eşsiz bir harita uzmanı
iyinin doğrunun güzelin kadastrosunu çıkaran

Sevgiyle nefret
eytişimsel bir güç kaynağıydı
onun poyrazla yarışan soluğunda.
Bir akşam altıncı katta bir balkonda
çocukluğunda oturdukları tek katlı evin
yosunlu kiremitlerini göstererek
"Notre Dame" demişti Sultani Fransızcasıyla.

TULUI SÖNMEZ

A man who kept gazing at the sky.
A falling plane?
or a person flying from a plane?
Perhaps what he sought was a letter
on the mountain top.

In the unemployment years
as a senior law student
with an out-of-work friend
he wrote an operetta
in the style of Muhlis Sabahattin.

Every time they looked at the Islands
from Takfor's tavern
they imagined a sea in flames;
so the neighbourhood elders spread the rumour
that, pouring petrol on the sea one night,
they set it alight.

His surviving friends can never forget him:
a long-distance runner
swift and enduring,
as well as a peerless expert cartographer
who produced a survey
of the good, the true, the beautiful.

Love and hatred
a dialectical power source in his breath
that rivalled the sharp north-easter.
One evening on a sixth-floor balcony
he pointed out the mossy tiles of a one-storeyed house,
his childhood home,
and called it 'Notre Dame' in his schoolboy French.

ŞU NEREDEN TÜTTÜĞÜ BİLİNMEYEN DUMAN

Belleğimde yüzünün parçalanan
değişik gölgelerini birleştiriyorum
iskeleye yanaşan geminin güvertesinde,
kulağımda eski bir şarkının yankısı sesler.

Geçmiş yeniden yaşanan bir ilkyaz
renk renk çiçekleri ve kelebekleriyle.
Avluda saksıları sulayan bir kadın
sözlerini unuttuğu bir türkü mırıldanıyor.

*

Neler anlatır şu karanlıkta uzayan ağaçlar
ve rüzgâr okşarken dallarda yapraklarını,
neden ürperir gecede yakamozlu suları
    dinlenen denizlerin?

Kulağı gecenin sessizliğinde,
gözleri göz kırpan yıldızlarda,
kimi arar yolunu şaşırmış bir uyurgezer
    mağarasında düşlerin?

*

Yağmurun ışıyan parmakları okşuyor
gecede cama dayadığın yüzünü.
Yarın güneş açtığında, toprak
baharın kokusunu yayacak ıslak otlara.

*

WHY THIS UNKNOWN SMOKY HAZE?

On the deck of a ship approaching harbour
I assemble the altered shadows of your face,
fragments in my memory,
the echo of an old song sounds in my ear.

A past spring revived
with its brilliant flowers and butterflies.
A woman watering flowerpots in the courtyard
hums a folksong, the words forgotten.

*

What stories are told by the trees that lengthen in the dark
and the wind that caresses their leaves on the boughs,
why does the phosphorescent water at night
            shiver when the sea's at rest?

His ear to the silence of night
his eyes on the twinkling stars,
a sleepwalker who lost his way searching for whom
            in the cave of dreams?

*

Shining fingers of rain caress your face
at night when you lean on the glass.
Tomorrow at sunrise the earth will be redolent
of damp grass and spring.

*

Nasılsa kuşların ezberindedir saçaklar
ve boşlukta kaybolup giden bir martının
süzülen kanatları yansıyacak
her yağmur damlasının lekesiz aynasında,

bir de şu nereden tüttüğü bilinmeyen duman.

Birds somehow retain the memory of eaves
and in every raindrop's spotless mirror
the gliding wings of a seagull lost in space
will be reflected,

so why this unknown smoky haze?

ŞEDDELERE DİKKAT MOLLA

Bir sesler dünyasında yaşıyoruz son günlerde:
Deniz Kızı Eftalya, Hamiyet Yüceses;
bazı geceler mehtap bizi sürüklüyor sularda.
Nicedir uzaklara uğurladığımız dostlardan
	haber almadan,
sabahları sessizliğe açılan pencerelerden
toprak damlarda düşlere sinen gölgeleri
	yorumluyoruz.

Seslere renkler karışıyor bazı geceler:
nerdeyse unutmuşken o yaz geçen günleri
yanan bir yalının alevlerini seyrediyoruz
	bir başka kıyıda.
Bir adam ormanla konuştuğunu sanıyor
ağaçların adlarını fısıldayarak;
bir kadın her akşam denize bakıyor durmadan
o saatlerde geri döneceklerini umarak
sabah karanlığında yaka paça götürülenlerin.

Çocukların gözleri göklerde, uçan kuşlarda,
kuş seslerinde kulakları. –
bir sesler dünyasında yaşıyoruz ne de olsa –
ve sararan bir fotoğraf koca dünya..

Bitmeyen bir yolculuk bu karabasan
	feryatla imdat arasında.

WATCH YOUR Ps AND Qs, MY FRIEND

These last days we've been living in a world of sounds;
Deniz Kızı Eftalya, Hamiyet Yüceses;
Some nights moonlight draws us out on the water.
How many friends we've seen off to distant lands,
         with no more news,
from windows opened to silence in the mornings
         we interpret
shadows that penetrate dreams in the earthen roofs.

Colours mingle with sounds some nights;
we watch those almost forgotten transient summer days
and the flames of a summer home on fire
         on another shore.
A man imagines he's talking with a forest
by whispering the names of trees;
a woman keeps looking at the sea every evening
hoping that those abducted in the dark of morning
will return at the same hour.

Children's eyes are on the skies, on flying birds,
their ears on birdsong –
we live after all in a world of sound –
and the huge world is a fading photograph.

This nightmare a never-ending journey
         between cries for help and rescue.

GÖKKUŞAĞININ ALTINDA

Bilinmez, bir beklediği var mıydı
o uzun yolculuğun kimsesiz bir durağında.
Yolda kalmış hurda bir kamyonun sönük
    farları gibiydi gözleri.
Karşı köprü altında yanıp sönerken
    dereye vuran gölge,
o kıraç yamaçta, umutsuzca bir umutla
    beklemişti habercisini.
"Gömdüm," dedi, " kendimden önce
    derinlerdeki izleri.
Artık hiçbir şeyim yok karanlığa katacak
    kendi yanılgılarımdan başka."

Elinden tutup yavaşça, dağılan sisin ötesinde
beliren adaları gösteriyorum şimdi karşı kıyıda.
Bir kadın çamaşır asıyor balkonda,
bir çocuk ıslık çalıyor, dalarken
batık bir gemiden saçlarına takılan
yosunları temizlerken.
Her şey çok yakındaymış gibi,
ayrıntılar şaşırtmıyor bizi
bu sessiz buluşmada.

Unutulmuş sesler yankılanıyor bulutlu dağların
    ardında.

UNDER THE RAINBOW

Was there an unknown person waiting
at a lonely stop on the long journey,
eyes like the dipped headlights of a rubbish truck
        at a standstill on the road.
Opposite under the bridge a shadow falls
        on the gleaming gutter,
On the arid slope he waits for the messenger,
        hope against hope.
'I buried', he said, 'before myself
        deeprooted tracks.
Now I have nothing to add to darkness
        but my own mistakes.'

Now, on the other bank, I gently take his hand
and show him islands appearing through shreds of mist.
A woman hangs a shirt on the balcony,
a youngster whistles, cleaning off seaweed
stuck to his hair from a sunken ship
when he dived.
Everything seemed very near,
no detail misled us
in this soundless meeting.

At the back of the cloudy mountains forgotten voices echo.

DÖNMEYEN

Bazen bir ağacın altına oturur susardık
dallarına konan kuşlarla dalgın
ve Bünyamin sabırla başlardı sorularına,
babamın uzun yol kaptanı oluşuyla ilgili.
Kutuplardan birine giderken
gemisi batmış, derdim,
severdim ortasından başlamaya o inanılmaz
      masala.
Işıyan gözlerini gözlerime diker,
soluksuz dinlerdi beni Bünyamin.
Donmuş bir denizde kaybolmuşlar, derdim,
o buzullar erimez mi hiç, diye sorardı,
ya da tayfalar, onları bekleyenler?
Bilinmez, söylenen yerde mi kaybolmuştur
      her kaybolan,
yoksa habersiz başka kıtalara mı gitmiştir?
Güneşin öbür yüzünü görmeye gitmişlerdir belki
o uzun eve dönüş yolculuğunu yarıda kesip.
Onlar da masallar dinlemişlerdir çocukluklarında,
büyülenmişlerdir o masallardaki ormanların
karanlığında gözleri parlayan kaplanlarla.
Bünyamin, ben, dallarda suskun kuşlar
kaybolur giderdik o ağacın altında.
Derken kurtulmak için buzlar altında kalan
o batık geminin ürpertisinden
bir çöl masalına başlardım akşam inerken.
Bilirdim çölleri de severdi Bünyamin,
çöllerde susuz kalan bedevileri,
dalgalanan kum tepelerini, akşamın alacasında
gölgeleri büyüyen develeri.

NO RETURN

Sometimes we'd sit silent under a tree
deep in thought with the birds perched on the boughs
and Bünyamin would patiently begin his questions
about my father's long voyage, when he was captain.
'His boat sank', I'd say,
'On its way to one of the Poles.'
I loved to begin that amazing story in the middle.
Bünyamin would fix his shining eyes on me
and listen, holding his breath.
'They were lost in a frozen sea,' I'd say,
'Did the icebergs never melt?', he'd ask
'And what of the sailors and those who waited?'
'Nobody knows if every lost soul was lost,
or did they go to other lands without telling?
Perhaps they went to see the sun's other face,
cutting in half the long journey home.
They had surely heard stories in their childhood,
and must have been bewitched by tigers
whose eyes gleamed in the darkness of fairytale forests.'
Bünyamin, I and the birds, silent on the branches,
would get lost beneath the tree.
Then as evening descended I'd embark on a desert tale
to save us from the shudder of a sunken ship
in the grip of ice.
I knew about deserts and Bünyamin loved
to hear of Bedouins who survived without water,
of undulating sandhills, and the camels
their shadows lengthening in the twilight.

Unutma, derdim, Bünyamin'e günün sonunda,
bu denizciler – kaptanlar, tayfalar –
öyle büyülü yerler görürler ki o uzak kıyılarda,
gözleri kamaşır, dönüş yolunu şaşırır,
evlerine hiç dönemezler.

At the day's end I'd say to Bünyamin, 'don't forget,
these sailors – captains and their crew –
would see such enchanted places in those distant lands
their eyes would be so dazzled they would lose their way
and could never go home again.'

AY IŞIĞINDA

Yıllarca birlikte yaşadıklarından
koparıp bir deliğe tıkmışlarsa seni,
yalnızca belleğinin özgürlüğüyle
kalakalmışsan birden,
kimseler bilemez hangi seslerin
çınlayacağını kulaklarında,
hangi güneşin doğarak
gözlerini kamaştıracağını
gökkuşağının ışıyan şavkıyla.

Nereden başlamalı diye düşünme artık,
nerede kalmıştık belki daha yerinde bir soru.
Elbette harikalar ülkesindesindir Alis'in,
ya da Cuma'yı arıyorsundur,
Robenson'un adasında;
 "mahzun yüzlü şövalye" de seni bekliyordur
 kurumuş bir çeşme başında
saldırmak için yel değirmenlerinin kanatlarına.
Her yere gidebilirsin şimdi
uçarak bir serçe gibi geceleri
demir parmaklıklar arasından
ay da çıkıp dolanmışsa orta yeri,
soluklanıp bulanık Fırat'ın bir kıyısında
varırsın belki de Buhara'ya, Semarkant'a
Hayyam'la Hasan Sabbah'ın buluşmasına.
Döndüğünde, seni bekliyor olacaktır
zaman denen Şehrazat ve bin bir geceden
uzun sürecektir gerçek makamındaki masallar.
Yeniden gün doğacak, uzayacak öğle saatleri,
sonra bir karabasan gibi çökecek bekleyiş
ve gene başlayacak düşlerde sorumluluklar.

BY MOONLIGHT

When they plucked you
from the life you'd led together for years
and stuffed you in a hole,
and you were paralyzed with fear,
only the freedom of memory left,
no one knew what voices would ring in your ears,
what sun would rise
and dazzle your sight
with the rainbow's luminous light.

Where to begin? Don't ask any more,
perhaps a better question is, where are we now?
Sure, you must be in Alice's wonderland
or looking for Man Friday
on Crusoe's island;
'the knight of the melancholy face' waits for you
by an empty fountain
to launch an attack on the wings of windmills.
Now you can go anywhere
and when the moon appears between iron railings
flying at night like a sparrow
revolving about you,
you'll take a deep breath and perhaps arrive
on a bank of the turgid Euphrates
in Bokhara or Samarkand
at the meeting of Omar Khayyam and Hasan Sabbah.
On your return Scheherazade, named time, will surely be waiting
with tales from a thousand and one nights in reality mode,
to divert you for ever.
Daybreak again, the afternoons will lengthen.
Then waiting will descend like a nightmare
and responsibilities in dreams will begin again.

EMEKLİ BİR ÇARKÇIBAŞI

Demek dağ çileği topluyordun dönmeden,
siyanür karışmadan kaynak sularına,
bu yıl ne çok kestane verdi sizin ağaçlar.
Ama unutma lüfer mevsimi başlamak üzere
    Boğaz'da,

Biliyorum, hiçbir şeyde gözün yoktur senin,
saatleri ayarlasan da olur, ayarlamasan da.
Kiraz Bibin tulum peyniri göndermiş köyden,
bir kavanoz da petekli bal çocuklar için.
Kış gelince, uzun uzun Keklik Pınarı'nı anlatırsın onlara,
Ağagil'in sarı kısrağını, üstüne sıçradığın Çerkez eyerini,
sıcaktan kuruyan çarıklarını nasıl yumuşattığını
derenin serin sularında.
Düşündüm de bir sabah erkenden yola çıksak,
şu ünlü yılanı arasak Alemdağ'da.
O bizi alıp Şehrazat'a götürse,
Şehrazat da sonu gelmeyen masallara uçursa
    Zümrüdüanka'nın duldasında.

A RETIRED CHIEF ENGINEER

So you were picking wild strawberries before you went home,
before the cyanide could mingle with the springs,
this year your trees gave so many chestnuts.
But don't forget the lüfer season just beginning
        on the Bosphorus.

I know you can't keep track of everything,
of whether you put the clocks right or not.
Your aunt Kiraz has sent you a skin of curd cheese from the village,
and an earthenware jar of honeycomb for the children.
When winter comes, you'll tell them lengthy tales
        of the Partridge Well
of Agagil's golden mare, his Circassian saddle you leapt on
and how you softened your leather sandals
dried up from the heat,
        in the stream's cool waters.

I thought we should set out early one morning
to look for the famous serpent on Alemdağ.
If it carried us off to Scheherazade,
Scheherazade could fly us to the stories with no end
        in the Phoenix's arbour.

HAYDAR HAYDAR

Suların bir zamanlar birikip dağıldığı alanda
çoğaldıkça köpüren, dalgalanan bu sevgi
gecenin göklerinden yıldızlara yansıyor
        kıvılcımlarıyla,
sonra da denizlerdeki yakamozlara,
ateşi sönmeyen ateşböcekleri hepsi.
Bir yaz gecesi düşüydü bu nicedir,
artık dört mevsim gerçeğine dönüştü
        Çarşı pazar özlenen.
Yepyeni bir dille konuşuyorlar direnirken,
yaprakların, çiçeklerin sesiyle sesleniyorlar
        birbirlerine
                su sesini bastıran.
Sabırla değiştiriyorlar bunaltıcı havayı,
değişen havayla insan da değişiyor, zaman da.

Ve dinmeyen kuş sesleri
        ağaçların dallarında.

HAYDAR HAYDAR

In the space where waters once ebbed and flowed,
this passion, rising and falling, effervescing as it grows,
is reflected in the sparkling stars
        of the night skies,
and in the phosphorescence of the seas,
in all the fireflies with their unquenched fire.
O what a summer night's dream that was,
the longed-for market transformed
        to a truth for all seasons.
They talk as they protest in a language completely new,
calling to each other with the voice of leaves,
        flowers,
                drowning the voice of water.
Gradually they alter the stifling air.
People and time change with the changing air.

Birdsong unceasing
        in the branches of trees.

MÜBADELE GÜNLERİ

Uzaktan karaya bakıyor, kara kara düşünüyorlardı:
bu yangın yerinde mi kuracaklardı yeni hayatlarını?
Bodur ağaçların arasında topçu bataryaları vardı,
zeytinlerle kaplı yamacın yarısı dinamitle atılmış
çimento fabrikası için öğütülmüştü. Kıyıda
bir iki balıkçı ağ onarıyordu. Demek yerlilerden de
denizi bilenler varmış diye sevindi yaşlılar.
Çocuklar şaşkındılar, onlara ne diyeceklerini
bilemiyordu kadınlar. Kıyıdakiler kuşkuyla karşıladılar
gelenleri, konuşmalarını yadırgadılar, komşuluk
geç başladı aralarında, onların pencerelerinde
teneke kutularda yetiştirdikleri sardunyalara, fesleğenlere
zamanla alıştılar. Yıllar geçti, zor yıllar.
Yeni gelenlerin dilleri de çalmıyor artık.

DAYS OF THE POPULATION EXCHANGE

Deep in sombre thought they gazed at the land ahead,
was it here, in this fire-ravaged place, they would begin new lives?
With artillery bunkers between squat bushes,
half a hillside covered with olives, blasted by dynamite,
fragments of rock ground to dust in a cement factory.
On shore a few fishermen were mending nets. The elders relieved
there were men among the locals who knew the sea,
children bewildered, women hardly knowing
what to tell them, and on shore the newcomers' alien speech
met with suspicion. Neighbourliness
came late between them. In time they got used
to geraniums and basil-plants reared in tins
on windowsills. Years passed, years of hardship,
and the newcomers' language no longer sounded strange.

III

FROM YALIOBA
YALIOBA'DAN

İçimden ezberimdeki türküleri söylüyorum sessizce,
bütün gece, seni beklerken.
"Etin ve belleğin parklarında" dolaşıyorum
kalabalıklarla.
Dağlardan inerek bahçeyi serinleten
suları düşünüyorum,
imbatla salınan çiçeklerin yapraklarını
o tenha bahçede
ve lacivert bir gece iniyor sulara yavaşça.

Birden,
sıçrayarak uyanırcasına
korkulu bir düşten,
gözleri alev alev yanan
o kaplan fırlıyor
karanlığın içinden.

*

Elimde, kovuğunda nice sessizlikler yankılanan
küçük bir deniz kabuğu,
yavaşça kulağıma götürüyorum
Li Po'un dizelerini dinlemek için.
Bir Budist keşişi tırmanıyor
bulutların örttüğü uzak bir tepeye –
Temmuzun on sekizi bugün,
ağustosböceklerini bekliyoruz
tenha bir meşelikte.
Anılar yaşlı kartallar gibi döneniyor
kara lekeler bırakarak
masmavi gökte.

*

YALIOBA DIARY II

I hum folksongs I know by heart under my breath,
     all night as I wait for you.
'In the parklands of memory and the flesh'[1] I roam
     with the crowds.
I think of streams that run down the mountains
     and cool the garden,
of flower petals fluttering in the Aegean breeze
     in that deserted garden
and a lapis lazuli night slowly descends on the waters.

Suddenly,
     like waking with a start
          from a frightful dream,
with flaming eyes
     the tiger springs
          from the heart of darkness.

    *

In my hand, so many silences echoing in its hollow
     a little seashell,
slowly I bring it to my ear
     to listen to Li Po's lines.
A Buddhist monk is climbing
     to a distant cloud-capped peak –
today on the eighteenth of July,
     in an empty oakwood
          we expect the cicadas.
Like old eagles memories circle
     leaving black specks
          in a deep blue sky.

    *

[1] A quotation from Mehmet Taner, a fellow poet.

Yalnız kendimize fısıldarız geçmişle ilgili
gizli özlemlerimizi:
Sevilla'yı düşün, 1964'te paskalya tatilinde,
otellerde yer bulamayıp
arabada sabahlamıştık beş kişi.
Çağrılınca her şeyi bırakıp giderdik o yıllar,
rüzgâr savururdu bir yerlere
buruşuk müsveddelerimizi.

We whisper our secret longings to do with the past
        only to ourselves:
think of Seville, the Easter holiday in 1964,
        the hotels were full
            and five of us spent the night in the car.
Those years when we'd take off on a whim, abandoning all,
        the wind would scatter our crumpled drafts
           in every direction.

İnsan baka baka
baktığı manzaraya dönüşür bazen
bir gün uçsuz bucaksız bir deniz yansır
    gözlerinde,
bir gece uzayıp giden bir çöl yıldızlar
    altında.

*

Seni anadilinde yazdığın o güzel dizeleri
üvey kardeşinmişim gibi yorumlamaya çalışıyorum
    kendimce,
renklerini soldurmamaya çiçeklerin.
Beni en çok zorlayan
    soluğunun düzeni.

*

Belki de Portekizli şair Pedro Tamen anlatmıştı
    Tarabya'da,
İstanbul'u andıran bir kıyı kentiymiş Lizbon,
inişli yokuşlu dar sokaklarında sarı tramvaylar
    dolaşan.
O akşam birlikte kendi dilimize çevirmeye
    çalışmıştık şu dizeyi:
"Küçük çocukları ısıran azgın bir köpektir
    zaman."

*

YALIOBA DIARY III

Sometimes if we look long and hard
we become the scene we contemplate
one day an infinite sea is reflected
        in our eyes,
One night under the stars a desert stretches
        without end.

        *

You and the lovely lines you write in your mother-tongue
like a half-brother I try to interpret
        in my own way,
without dimming the glow of your flowers.
What is hardest for me
        is the pulse of your breath.

        *

It was probably the Portuguese poet Pedro Tamen who described
        in Tarabya
Lisbon as a city by the sea like Istanbul,
its yellow tramcars rambling uphill and down
        the narrow streets.
Together one evening we tried to translate in our own tongue
        the line:
"Time is a rabid dog that bites
        the young."

        *

Bugün de kıyısındayım denizin,
Rumlardan kalma yıkık kalenin
    yamacında,
Belki de sendendir diyedir imbatla gelen
    bu serinlik.
Dönsem, su serpsem bahçedeki kayrak
    taşlarına,
çardağın altı da serinlese akşamsefaları
    açarken.

*

Gün batarken yaklaşıyorduk köye,
    atlarımız yorgun.
Bakıyorum, ne rüzgâr, ne yağmur,
ne de dallarda alabildiğine devinen
    yapraklar.
Köye bir helalleşme dönüşü bu askere
    gitmeden.
Sonra üç yıl Sarıkamış, karlı kışlar,
    mektuplar, mektuplar.

Böyle nice yolculuklara çıktım,
büsbütün dönmüş de sayılmam
gittiğim çoğu yerden.

Today too I'm on the shore of a sea,
on the slopes of a ruined fortress,
        Byzantine remains,
perhaps this cooling breeze from the western seas
        is sent by you.
When I return and sprinkle water on the burning
        stones in the garden,
the arbour will cool and the evening-wonders
        open.

        *

At sunset we were nearing the village,
        our horses weary.
I look, there's no wind, no rain,
and on the branches, unbelievably, no leaves
        stirring.
This is a return and farewell
        before enlisting.
Then three years in Sarıkamiş, snowy winters,
        and letters, letters.

I've set out on many a journey,
but have I ever wholly returned
from most of the places I've been?

Dağları aşıp güneye indiğinde, kurumuş dere yataklarını göreceksin
    kıyıya yaklaştıkça.
İda'nın kırkayağı andıran çok tepeli yamaçlarında yeryüzüyle
    gökyüzünü birleştiren çamlar varmış eskiden,
düzlük bahçelerde yetişen çeşit çeşit meyveler ve sebzeler.
Ozanın bol pınarlı, vahşi hayvanlar anası dediği İda'nın eteklerinde
daha çok arabalarıyla oradan hızla geçen vahşi insanlara rastlarsın
    bugün.

*

Geniş ağızlı bir körfeze dökülen Mıhlı Çayı'nın yukarısındaki
    eski değirmendeyiz şimdi, bir düğünde.
Güvey ulu çınarlar altında akan soğuk sulara dalıyor
    mutluluğun peşinde,
gelin duvağını düzeltiyor adalar denizine bakarak.

*

Bir zamanlar ünlü Akhileus'un yerle bir etmekle övündüğü
    bu toprakları
şimdi başka barbarlar yağmalıyorlar. Ağlayan sızlayan
kadınların iniltileri duyulurmuş bol pınarlı koyaklarda
    o yıllar,
şimdi Assos'un mermer sütunlu batık limanına duyulan
    hayranlık yankılanıyor sularda.

*

YALIOBA DIARY IV

Heading south over the mountains, the closer to shore
      the more dry riverbeds you'll see.
Once on Ida's many-crested slopes were pinetrees
      uniting earth and sky,
and fertile orchards, kitchen gardens flourishing on the plain.
Today on the foothills of Ida – the poet called her
mother of wild beasts and many streams –
you'll meet instead a horde of crazy drivers hurtling from the scene.

    *

Now we're at a wedding in the old mill above the Mıhlı Stream
      that falls to the wide-armed gulf.
Pursuing happiness, the bridegroom dives into cold waters that pour
      under lofty planetrees,
while the bride surveys the sea of islands and adjusts her veil.

    *

Now other barbarians despoil the lands once famous for Achilles
who boasted he'd delete the lot without a trace.
    Long ago
in the well-watered valleys were heard the laments
      of women weeping in pain.
Now we hear wonder echoing in the waters
      for Assos' sunken harbour with its marble columns.

    *

Gece sessiz. Burayı bırakıp gidenler nasılsa çok bekletmeden
dönerler sanıyordu geride kalanlar,
Oysa gece gündüz sürüp gitti bu uzun bekleyiş.
Geride kaldı bir süre mektuplarla oyalandıkları günler,
çünkü mektupların da arkası gelmedi,
saçları ağardı bekleyenlerin, gidenler dönmediler,
zamanla unutuldular.

Night and silence. Those who remained imagined
      that somehow the departed would soon return,
but the long waiting lasted days and nights.
Some days they amused themselves for a while with letters,
      the letters came to nothing.
The hair of the waiting ones grew white, the departed never came back,
      in time forgotten.

SU SESİ

Önce Kar Kitabı'nda yazılıydı adları,
baharda karlar eriyince,
    kaybolup gittiler –
oysa doğanın ezberindeydi o adlar,
cemrelerle yeniden belirdiler.
Kimi sabahın çiğiyle çiçeklerde,
kimi akşamın kızıllığında, ufukta.

*

Haziran sonu
poyrazla başladıydı yaz,
haftalarca hiç dinmeden
kayaları dövdü dalgalar.
Homeros'un sesi Tenedos'ta
martı çığlıklarıyla
    rüzgârın sesine karıştı.

*

Temmuz da sona ermek üzere –
Rüzgârın görünmeyen salıncağında
    titriyor kavağın yaprakları,
azmağın körfeze karışan suları
    öğle sıcağında bile dipdiri.

THE VOICE OF WATER

Their names were first inscribed in the Book of Snow,
as the snows melted in spring
      they disappeared –
but imprinted in nature's memory, those names
reappeared in the warmth of spring.
Some in flowers dewy with morning,
some in evening's glow on the horizon.

   *

The end of June
summer had begun with the north-east wind,
with no let-up for weeks
waves beat on the rocks.
On Tenedos Homer's voice
      mixed with the sound of wind
and the screams of seagulls.

   *

And near the end of July –
in the wind's invisible cradle
      poplar leaves tremble,
the waters of swollen rivers churn in the bay
      alive with power even in the heat of noon.

ŞAFAKTA

Küçük dayımla balığa çıktığımız geceler
hiç sabah olmasın isterdim –
balıklar uyuyorlarsa, hiç uyanmasınlar
    düşlerinden.
O zaman yalnız yorumlayamadığımız
    düşlerle döneriz, derdi dayım.
Biz de düşlerimizi o yorumsuz düşlere katıp
öyle dönerdik Müsellim Boğazı'ndan
    tanyeri ağarırken.

AT DAYBREAK

The nights I went fishing with my younger uncle
I'd wish that morning would never arrive –
if the fish were asleep, that they might not awake
    from their dreams.
Then, my uncle would say, we'd return with only a catch of dreams
    we can't interpret.
So adding our own to those impenetrable dreams
we'd go home from Müsellim Channel
    as dawn was breaking.

ZURBARAN

Karanlığın içindeki kızıllık.
Her türlü yeşillik de soluyor
kaybolup gidince gözden
ve sona eriyor kamaşma
ışıkla gölgeler arasında.

Hatırlıyor musun Nurganalı Ali'yi?
onun Lorca'yla ilgili anılarını
Sevilla'dan, Cadiz'den?
Soyut resimler yapardı bir ara
Selim Turan'ı andıran.

ZURBARAN

Red glow within darkness.
And every tone of green fades
disappearing from sight lost
and between light and shade
radiance reaches its peak.

Do you remember Ali of Nurgana?
his memories of Lorca
from Seville and from Cadiz?
Now and then he painted abstracts
that reminded us of Selim Turan.

p. 63 'Tului Sönmez':
In the last line the poet makes a private joke typical of Tului. 'Notre Dame' puns with the Turkish 'dam' (roof, small house) and refers to Galatasaray Lyceé, the school from which Tului Sönmez graduated.

p. 69 'Watch your Ps and Qs My Friend':
The English title is a free translation of the Turkish, which quotes a young mullah's advice to a friend about to be examined by very strict *hodjas*. The poem refers obliquely to some Rumeli people who mispronounce their consonants and is an indirect comment on the misunderstandings between different groups in contemporary Turkey. It also implies the impossibility of understanding the complexities of the modern world.

p. 81 'Haydar Haydar':
Haydar Haydar is the title of a folksong, sung during the Gezi Park protest in Taksim Square in the summer of 2013, challenging the police force and their methods of dealing with the uprising.

BIOGRAPHICAL NOTES

Cevat Çapan was born in Kocaeli in 1933, attended Robert College in Istanbul and went on to read English at at the University of Cambridge. After graduating in 1956, he worked as a Programme Assistant in the BBC Turkish Section for a year before returning to Turkey to take up a post in the Department of English Language and Literature in the Faculty of Literature at Istanbul University. He became an Associate Professor in 1968 and full Professor in 1975. From 1980-1996, he was Professor of Drama in Mimar Sinan University, during which time he went to New York on a Fulbright scholarship. In 1996 he moved to Yeditepe University where he was Dean in the Faculty of Literature and Professor of English and Drama for 16 years. He also taught at Bosphorus University, Anadolu University, and Marmara University as Visiting Professor. He is currently Professor of Drama at the Haliç Uhiversity.

Cevat Çapan's poetry first appeared in numerous journals and in 1985, his first collection *Dön Güvercin Dön* (Return to Güvercin Dön) was published. Since then, seven more collections have appeared, the most recent in 2013. He has edited anthologies of modern Greek, English and American poetry and is the author of a number of books of literary criticism on contemporary English and Irish drama. As a translator, he has translated John Berger's *A Seventh Man, Photocopies*, and *To the Wedding*; the poetry of Seferis, Ritsos, Cavafy, W. B. Yeats, Pessoa, Mandelstam, Ferlinghetti, Carlos Durummond de Andrade, Raymond Carver, Ungaretti and Tomas Tranströmer; and the plays of O'Casey, Whiting, Wesker, and Athol Fugard. His own poetry has been translated into English (*Where are You Susie Petschek*, Arc, 2000), Persian (2015) and Bulgarian (2016).

Cevat Çapan has received a number of prestigious literary awards – the Behçet Necatigil Poetry Award, 1986, the Homeros Culture and Art Award, 2007, the Altın Portakal Şiir Ödülü (Golden Orange Poetry Award), 2008 and the Mersin City Literature Award, 2015.

Cevat Çapan is married with three children.

RUTH CHRISTIE was born and educated in Scotland, and after graduating from from the University of St Andrews, taught English for two years in Turkey, later studying Turkish language and literature at London University. For several years she taught English literature to American undergraduates resident in London. With Saliha Paker she translated a Turkish novel by Latife Tekin (Marion Boyars, 1993) and in collaboration with Richard McKane a selection of the poems of Oktay Rifat (Rockingham Press 1993). A major collection of Nâzim Hikmet's poetry, again with Richard McKane, was published by Anvil Press in 2002. In 2004 *In the Temple of a Patient God*, her translations from the Turkish of Bejan Matur, was published by Arc Publications in its 'Visible Poets' translation series.

Recent translations include a major collection, *Poems of Oktay Rifat*, co-translated with Richard McKane (Anvil,2007), which was runner-up in the Popescu Poetry Prize; a translation (in collaboration with Selçuk Berilgen) of Selçuk Altun's novel *Songs My Mother Never Taught Me*, (Telegram, 2008); and a translation (with Selçuk Berilgen) of Bejan Matur's *How Abraham Abandoned Me* (Arc, 2012) which was a Poetry Book Society Recommended Translation.

RONALD TAMPLIN was born in London in 1935, educated at Sir George Monoux Grammar School, Walthamstow and at Merton College, Oxford. He taught English Literature at the universities of Auckland and Waikato in New Zealand from 1961-1967 before moving back to the UK to join the staff of the University of Exeter, where he taught until 1990. After retiring to devote more time to writing, he held visiting professorships at the universities of Rennes, France and Bilkent, Ankara, Turkey and was also Honorary University Fellow at the University of Exeter until 2006. He has published a number of books of literary criticism and his academic articles have appeared in conference proceedings, as contributions to books, and in many journals. His poetry has appeared in many magazines – mainly in the

United Kingdom but also in Australia, Canada, France, Ireland, Italy, New Zealand, Turkey, and the USA – in anthologies, and in three collections, the most recent, *Checkpoint* (2010).

Among his published translations of poetry are sections of an ongoing modern verse version of the fourteenth-century Middle English poem *Piers Plowman* which have appeared in several anthologies, and, in collaboration, poems from a number of Turkish poets including Enis Batur, Ilhan Berk, and Edip Cansever.

ARC PUBLICATIONS
publishes translated poetry in bilingual editions
in these series:

ARC TRANSLATIONS
Series Editor Jean Boase-Beier

'VISIBLE POETS'
Series Editor Jean Boase-Beier

ARC CLASSICS –
NEW TRANSLATIONS OF GREAT POETS OF THE PAST
Series Editor Jean Boase-Beier

ARC ANTHOLOGIES IN TRANSLATION
Series Editor Jean Boase-Beier

NEW VOICES FROM EUROPE & BEYOND
(anthologies)
Series Editor Alexandra Büchler

Details of these series can be found on the
Arc Publications website at
arcpublications.co.uk